Will Rick Get His Wish?

by Nat Gabriel
illustrated by Bridget Starr Taylor

Scott Foresman

Editorial Offices: Glenview, Illinois • New York, New York
Sales Offices: Reading, Massachusetts • Duluth, Georgia
Glenview, Illinois • Carrollton, Texas • Menlo Park, California

How many fish can Rick see?

Rick can see six fish.

Rick can see big fish.

Rick can see little fish.

Why do the fish sink?
Are they sick?

They are not sick.

They are quick!

Rick has a wish.

Will Rick get his wish?

Rick did get his wish.

Rick has one fish!